Sarah Lawrie for Aegis Production
for the Finborough Theatre prese

The world premiere

SCROUNGER
by Athena Stevens

First performed at the Finborough Theatre as a staged reading as part of *Vibrant 2019 – A Festival of Finborough Playwrights*: Monday, 1 July 2019.

First performance at the Finborough Theatre: Tuesday, 7 January 2020.

SCROUNGER

by Athena Stevens

Cast in order of speaking

Scrounger	**Athena Stevens**
P.A.	**Leigh Quinn**

Here. Now.

There will be no interval.

Director	**Lily McLeish**
Designer	**Anna Reid**
Lighting Designer	**Anthony Doran**
Sound Designer	**Julian Starr**
Stage Manager	**Lucy Barter**
Assistant Director	**Wiebke Green**
Production Manager	**Ian Taylor**
Producer	**Sarah Lawrie**

Please see front of house notices or ask an usher for an exact running time.

Please turn your mobile phones off - the light they emit can also be distracting.

Our patrons are respectfully reminded that, in this intimate theatre, any noise such as the rustling of programmes, food packaging or talking may distract the actors and your fellow audience members.

We regret there is no admittance or re-admittance to the auditorium whilst the performance is in progress.

Athena Stevens | Scrounger / Playwright

Athena Stevens is a Playwright on Attachment at the Finborough Theatre, where her productions as actor and writer have included *Scrounger* as part of *Vibrant 2019 – A Festival of Finborough Playwrights*, *Genie* as part of *Vibrant 2017 – A Festival of Finborough Playwrights* and *Schism* (which subsequently transferred to the Park Theatre). For her work on *Schism*, Athena was nominated for an OffWestEnd Award for Best Female Performance in a Play and an Olivier Award.

Athena Stevens is a writer, performer and director. She is a Creative Council member and Associate Artist at Shakespeare's Globe.

Writing includes *Reluctant Spirit* (BBC Radio 3) and *Hello to the Trolls*, a new commission from the National Youth Theatre. She is a BBC Writers Access Group member, a former writer on attachment with the National Theatre Studio and recently completed a screen version of her series *Recompense* as part of the Channel 4 Screenwriters Programme.

Acting includes understudying for *A Day in the Death of Joe Egg* (Trafalgar Studios), Juliet in *Redefining Juliet* (Royal Shakespeare Company at the Barbican Theatre) and Lady Macbeth (RADA).

Writing and acting her own work includes *The Amazing Vancetti Sisters* (Tristan Bates Theatre) and *Dark Night of The Soul* (Shakespeare's Globe).

Forthcoming productions include directing and curating *Notes to the Forgotten She-Wolves* (Sam Wanamaker Season 2020 at Shakespeare's Globe).

Film and Television include the feature documentary *Day of Small Things* (Channel 4), the short film *The Conference* (BBC) and three web series for YouTube.

She is currently launching the self-advocacy platform *Make Your Own Damn Tea*, is a Huffington Post contributor and is completing her first non-fiction book. Athena is also a TEDx speaker, and Equality in the Media Spokesperson for the Women's Equality Party.

Born in Chicago, she now lives in London. Athena was born with athetoid cerebral palsy.

Leigh Quinn | P.A.

Trained at Bristol Old Vic Theatre School.

Theatre includes *The Crucible*, *A Little Night Music* (Storyhouse, Chester), *Troilus and Cressida*, *Richard II*, *Henry IV Parts I and II*, *Henry V*, *The Famous Victories of Henry V*, *Two Gentlemen of Verona* (Royal Shakespeare Company, UK, China and New York), *Pride and Prejudice* (Open Air Theatre, Regent's Park), *The Low Road* (Royal Court Theatre) and *Dancing at Lughnasa* (Tobacco Factory, Bristol).

Television and Film includes *Year of the Rabbit*, *Case Histories*, *Shakespeare Live!*, *All the Milkman's Children*, *Three Lives*, *Best of Men* and *8 Minutes Idle*.

Lily McLeish | Director

Lily McLeish is a British-German theatre director. She read English Literature and Art History at the University of Cologne. She is a creative fellow of the Royal Shakespeare Company, long-term associate director to Katie Mitchell on productions across Europe, and director of Fizzy Sherbet, a new writing initiative for women playwrights.

Direction includes *While You Are Here* (DanceEast and The Place), *Schism* (Park Theatre), *The White Bike* (The Space), *Unlocked* (Glenside Hospital Museum for alldaybreakfast, Bristol), *A Colder Water Than Here*, awarded the Origins Award For Outstanding New Work (Vaults Festival), *She Echoes* (University of Northampton), *Three Lives* (Fringe Arts, Bath), *Housekeeping* (Southwark Playhouse), *Absence* (The Young Vic), *This Despised Love* (Royal Shakespeare Company Fringe), *Old Times* (Artheater, Cologne) and *Footfalls* (Severins-Burg-Theater, Cologne).

Associate Direction includes *Anatomie eines Suizids*, *Bluets*, *Schlafende Männer*, *4.48 Psychosis*, *Reisende auf einem Bein*, *Happy Days* (Deutsches Schauspielhaus, Hamburg), *Orlando*, *Schatten*, *Ophelias Zimmer* (Schaubühne, Berlin), *Norma Jeane Baker of Troy* (The Shed, New York), *Anatomy of a Suicide*, *Ophelias Zimmer* (Royal Court Theatre) and *La Maladie de la Mort* (Théâtre des Bouffes du Nord, Paris).

Assistant Direction includes *When We Have Sufficiently Tortured Each Other*, *Cleansed*, *The Beaux' Stratagem* (National Theatre), *The Two Gentlemen of Verona* (Royal Shakespeare Company), *Ariadne auf Naxos* (Festival d'Aix en Provence), *Lucia di Lammermoor* (Royal Opera House, Covent Garden), *The Forbidden Zone* (Salzburg Festspiele and Schaubühne, Berlin), *Wunschloses Unglück* (Burgtheater, Vienna), *Alles Weitere Kennen Sie Aus Dem Kino* (Deutsches Schauspielhaus, Hamburg), *Say It With Flowers* (Hampstead Theatre), *The Yellow Wallpaper* (Schaubühne, Berlin), and *Reise durch die Nacht*, *Ringe des Saturn*, *Hundsprozesse* (Schauspiel, Cologne).

Anna Reid | Designer

Productions at the Finborough Theatre include *I'm Gonna Pray for You So Hard*.

Trained at Wimbledon College of Art.

Design includes *Dust* (New York Theatre Workshop), *Cash Cow*, *Paradise*, *The Hoes* (Hampstead Theatre), *The Sweet Science of Bruising* (Wilton's Music Hall), *Our Country's Good*, *A Midsummer Night's Dream* (Tobacco Factory Theatre), *Soft Animals*, *Fury* (Soho Theatre), *Twelfth Night*, *Collective Rage*, *Dear Brutus*, *The Cardinal, School Play* (Southwark Playhouse), *Rasheeda Speaking* (Trafalgar Studios), *Mary's Babies*, *Dry Land* (Jermyn Street Theatre), *Schism* (Park Theatre), *Grotty* (Bunker Theatre), *Tiny*

Dynamite (Old Red Lion Theatre), *Rattle Snake* (Live Theatre Newcastle, York Theatre Royal and Soho Theatre), *The Kitchen Sink, Jumpers for Goalposts* (Coliseum Theatre, Oldham), *Arthur's World* (Bush Theatre) and *Hamlet* (Riverside Studios). Anna was selected to represent the UK as an emerging designer at World Stage Design 2017.

Anthony Doran | Lighting Designer

Trained in Lighting Design at Rose Bruford College.

Lighting Designs include Katie Mitchell's cinema productions of *Orlando* (Schaubühne, Berlin), *La Maladie de la Mort* (Théâtre des Bouffes du Nord, Paris), *Shadows (Eurydice Speaks)* (Schaubühne, Berlin), *Bluets* (Deutsches Schauspielhaus, Hamburg) and *Norma Jeane Baker of Troy* (The Shed, New York). Lighting design for dance includes *Psychoacoustic* and *Asymptote* (Jack Philp Dance).

Associate Lighting Designs include collaborating with Jack Knowles on *Reisende auf einem Bein (Traveling on One Leg)*. Anthony has also toured extensively as a re-lighter and worked on numerous fashion events.

Julian Starr | Sound Designer

Productions at the Finborough Theatre include *A Winning Hazard, After Dark* and *The Wind of Heaven*.

Trained at the Australian National Institute of Dramatic Arts.

Sound Designs include *ZOG* (UK Tour), *Othello* (Union Theatre), *Cry Havoc, Hell Yes I'm Tough Enough, Martha, Josie and the Chinese Elvis* (Park Theatre), *Violet* (UK Tour), *Aisha* for which he received an OffWestEnd nomination for Best Sound Design (London Tour), *The Orchestra* (Omnibus Theatre), *Alice In Slasherland* (Old Fitz Theatre, Sydney), *White Noise* (Vaults Festival), *The Boy Under the Christmas Tree* (King's Head Theatre), *Tiger Under My Skin* (Bloomsbury Theatre), *The Giant Killers* (UK Tour), *Eris* (Bunker Theatre), *Gulliver Returns* (UK Tour), *You Only Live Forever* (Soho Theatre and UK Tour), *Surf Seance* (Sydney Arts Festival), *The Comedy of Errors, Pericles* (UK and Czech Republic Tour), *Precious Little* (Brockley Jack Theatre), *The Good Scout* (Above the Stag and Edinburgh Festival), *The Shifting Heart* (Seymour Centre, Sydney), *Untold* (Playhouse Theatre Sydney), *Kapow* (Kings Cross Theatre, Sydney), *Telescope* (Old Fitz Theatre, Sydney), *Best Before* (Sydney Fringe Festival) and *The Shadow Box* (Old Fitz Theatre, Sydney).

Sound Design Assistant and Associate Designer includes *Mamma Mia! the Musical* (Capital Theatre, Sydney), *Disney's Aladdin The Musical* (Queensland QPAC, and Assistant Sound Designer to Australasia Sound Associate), *Talk, Richard III* (Sydney Opera House), *The Royal Edinburgh Military Tattoo* (Edinburgh Castle) and *An Inspector Calls* (UK and Ireland Tour).

Lucy Barter | Stage Manager

Stage Management includes Company Stage Manager for *Whilst You Are Here*, directed by Lily McLeish (West End and UK Tour), *The Life I Lead* (Jonathan Church Productions and Northcott Theatre, Exeter) and *Mr Stink* (Chickenshed Theatre). She has toured with comedians Miles Jupp, Punt and Dennis, Ayesha Hazarika and Sandi Toksvig. Production Management for film includes independent feature *Above the Clouds*, which is currently screening at film festivals worldwide. Lucy regularly manages Amnesty International UK's float at London Pride and coordinates the firework display at Alexandra Palace each November.

Production Acknowledgements

Ms Stevens' Assistant | **Olivia Wakeford**

Production Coordinator for Aegis Productions | **Sacha Billingham**

Production Accountant | **Annegret Kuhnigk**

We would like to thank Georgie Staight.

Aegis Productions Ltd is a private limited company, registered in England and Wales under company number 07567099. Registered office address is 95 Brandon Street, London, England, SE17 1DY.

THEATRE

118 Finborough Road, London SW10 9ED
admin@finboroughtheatre.co.uk | www.finboroughtheatre.co.uk

"Probably the most influential fringe theatre in the world."
Time Out

"Under Neil McPherson, possibly the most unsung of all major artistic directors in Britain, the Finborough has continued to plough a fertile path of new plays and rare revivals that gives it an influence disproportionate to its tiny 50-seat size."
Mark Shenton, *The Stage*

"The mighty little Finborough which, under Neil McPherson, continues to offer a mixture of neglected classics and new writing in a cannily curated mix."
Lyn Gardner, *The Stage*

"The tiny but mighty Finborough"
Ben Brantley, *The New York Times*

Founded in 1980, the multi-award-winning Finborough Theatre presents plays and music theatre, concentrated exclusively on vibrant new writing and unique rediscoveries from the 19th and 20th centuries.

Our programme is unique – we never present work that has been seen anywhere in London during the last 25 years. Behind the scenes, we continue to discover and develop a new generation of theatre makers – most notably through our annual festival of new writing, now in its eleventh consecutive year – *Vibrant – A Festival of Finborough Playwrights*.

Despite remaining completely unsubsidised, the Finborough Theatre has an unparalleled track record for attracting the finest talent who go on to become leading voices in British theatre. Under Artistic Director Neil McPherson, it has discovered some of the UK's most exciting new playwrights including Laura Wade, James Graham, Mike Bartlett, Jack Thorne, Alexandra Wood, Nicholas de Jongh and Anders Lustgarten; and directors including Tamara Harvey, Robert Hastie, Blanche McIntyre, Kate Wasserberg and Sam Yates.

Artists working at the theatre in the 1980s included Clive Barker, Rory Bremner, Nica Burns, Kathy Burke, Ken Campbell, Jane Horrocks and Claire Dowie. In the 1990s, the Finborough Theatre first became known for new writing including Naomi Wallace's first play *The War Boys*; Rachel Weisz in David Farr's *Neville Southall's Washbag*; four plays by Anthony Neilson including *Penetrator* and *The Censor*, both of which transferred to the Royal Court Theatre; and new plays by Richard Bean, Lucinda Coxon, David Eldridge, Tony Marchant and Mark Ravenhill. New writing development included the premieres of modern classics such as Mark Ravenhill's *Shopping and F***king*, Conor McPherson's *This Lime Tree Bower*, Naomi Wallace's *Slaughter City* and Martin McDonagh's *The Pillowman*.

Since 2000, new British plays have included Laura Wade's London debut *Young Emma*, commissioned for the Finborough Theatre; two one-woman shows by Miranda Hart; James Graham's *Albert's Boy* with Victor Spinetti; Sarah Grochala's *S27*; Athena Stevens' *Schism* which was nominated for an Olivier Award; and West End transfers for Joy Wilkinson's *Fair*; Nicholas de Jongh's *Plague Over England*; Jack Thorne's *Fanny and Faggot*; Neil McPherson's Olivier Award nominated *It Is Easy To Be Dead*; and Dawn King's *Foxfinder*.

UK premieres of foreign plays have included plays by Brad Fraser, Lanford Wilson, Larry Kramer, Tennessee Williams, the English premiere of Robert McLellan's Scots language classic, *Jamie the Saxt*; and three West End transfers – Frank McGuinness' *Gates of Gold* with William Gaunt and John Bennett; and Craig Higginson's *Dream of the Dog* with Dame Janet Suzman.

Rediscoveries of neglected work – most commissioned by the Finborough Theatre – have included the first London revivals of Rolf Hochhuth's *Soldiers* and *The Representative*; both parts of Keith Dewhurst's *Lark Rise to Candleford*; *The Women's War*, an evening of original suffragette plays; *Etta Jenks* with Clarke Peters and Daniela Nardini; Noël Coward's first play *The Rat Trap*; Emlyn Williams' *Accolade*; Lennox Robinson's *Drama at Inish* with Celia Imrie and Paul O'Grady; John Van Druten's *London Wall* which transferred to St James' Theatre; and J. B. Priestley's *Cornelius* which transferred to a sell out Off Broadway run in New York City.

Music Theatre has included the new (premieres from Grant Olding, Charles Miller, Michael John LaChuisa, Adam Guettel, Andrew Lippa, Paul Scott Goodman, and Adam Gwon's *Ordinary Days* which transferred to the West End) and the old (the UK premiere of Rodgers and Hammerstein's *State Fair* which also transferred to the West End), and the acclaimed 'Celebrating British Music Theatre' series.

The Finborough Theatre won *The Stage* Fringe Theatre of the Year Award in 2011, *London Theatre Reviews'* Empty Space Peter Brook Award in 2010 and 2012, swept the board with eight awards at the 2012 OffWestEnd Awards, and was nominated for an Olivier Award in 2017 and 2019. Artistic Director Neil McPherson was awarded the Critics' Circle Special Award for Services to Theatre in 2019.

It is the only unsubsidised theatre ever to be awarded the Channel 4 Playwrights Scheme bursary eleven times.

www.finboroughtheatre.co.uk

FINBOROUGH THEATRE

118 Finborough Road, London SW10 9ED
admin@finboroughtheatre.co.uk | www.finboroughtheatre.co.uk

The Finborough Theatre has the support of the Channel 4 Playwrights' Scheme, sponsored by Channel 4 Television and supported by The Peggy Ramsay Foundation.

The Finborough Theatre gratefully acknowledges the support for its 2019-2020 season from Bill Kenwright whose generous donation to the Finborough Theatre has made this year's work possible.

The FinboroughForum is supported by the George Goetchius and Donald Howarth Society of Friend's Awards.

THE FINBOROUGH THEATRE RECEIVES NO FUNDING FROM THE ROYAL BOROUGH OF KENSINGTON AND CHELSEA.

The Finborough Theatre is a member of the Independent Theatre Council, the Society of Independent Theatres, Musical Theatre Network, The Friends of Brompton Cemetery and The Earl's Court Society; and supports #time4change's Mental Health Charter.

Supported by

Mailing
Email admin@finboroughtheatre.co.uk or give your details to our Box Office staff to join our free email list.

Feedback
We welcome your comments, complaints and suggestions. Write to Finborough Theatre, 118 Finborough Road, London SW10 9ED or email us at admin@finboroughtheatre.co.uk

Playscripts
Many of the Finborough Theatre's plays have been published and are on sale from our website.

On Social Media

 www.facebook.com/FinboroughTheatre

 www.twitter.com/finborough

 finboroughtheatre.tumblr.com

 www.instagram.com/finboroughtheatre

 www.youtube.com/user/finboroughtheatre

Friends
The Finborough Theatre is a registered charity. We receive no public funding, and rely solely on the support of our audiences. Please do consider supporting us by becoming a member of our Friends of the Finborough Theatre scheme. There are four categories of Friends, each offering a wide range of benefits.

Richard Tauber Friends – David and Melanie Alpers. David Barnes. Mark Bentley. Kate Beswick. Deirdre Feehan. Michael Forster. Jennifer Jacobs. Paul and Lindsay Kennedy. Martin and Wendy Kramer. John Lawson. Kathryn McDowall.

William Terriss Friends – Paul Guinery. Janet and Leo Liebster. Ros and Alan Haigh.

Adelaide Neilson Friends – Philip G Hooker.

Smoking is not permitted in the auditorium and the use of cameras and recording equipment is strictly prohibited. In accordance with the requirements of the Royal Borough of Kensington and Chelsea:

1. The public may leave at the end of the performance by all doors and such doors must at that time be kept open.

2. All gangways, corridors, staircases and external passageways intended for exit shall be left entirely free from obstruction whether permanent or temporary.

3. Persons shall not be permitted to stand or sit in any of the gangways intercepting the seating or to sit in any of the other gangways.

The Finborough Theatre is licensed by the Royal Borough of Kensington and Chelsea to The Steam Industry, a registered charity and a company limited by guarantee. Registered in England and Wales no. 3448268. Registered Charity no. 1071304. Registered Office: 118 Finborough Road, London SW10 9ED.

The Steam Industry was founded by Phil Willmott in 1992. It comprises two strands to its work: the Finborough Theatre (under Artistic Director Neil McPherson); and The Phil Willmott Company (under Artistic Director Phil Willmott) which presents productions throughout London as well as annually at the Finborough Theatre.

Athena Stevens

SCROUNGER

OBERON BOOKS
LONDON

WWW.OBERONBOOKS.COM

First published in 2020 by Oberon Books Ltd
521 Caledonian Road, London N7 9RH
Tel: +44 (0) 20 7607 3637 / Fax: +44 (0) 20 7607 3629
e-mail: info@oberonbooks.com
www.oberonbooks.com

PB ISBN: 9781786828958
E ISBN: 9781786828941

Cover image: Lily McLeish

Printed and bound in the UK.

Visit www.oberonbooks.com to read more about all our books and to buy them. You
will also find features, author interviews and news of any author events, and you can
sign up for e-newsletters and be the first to hear about our new releases.

Printed on FSC accredited paper

10 9 8 7 6 5 4 3 2 1

To anyone who has ever been told
that they should 'be more like Gandhi'.

Introduction by Athena Stevens

Part of being a creative person who happens to have a disability, is that everyone thinks something you've encountered should be written as a show. You have a broken lift in your building? Write a show about it! You've been forced to end a friendship because that other person won't listen when you say their actions are discriminatory? Time to write a script! Have a situation where you increasingly feel like you're in some sort of Ionesco play with no discernible way out? Get writing!

Isn't it funny how we depend on the victims to come up with the words and form to make us, as a society, understand the trauma we thrust upon them?

Oh, and be sure to do it as a solo show. On a low budget. That way, if you're very lucky, you might get to tour to community centres and libraries.

That way, other performers won't have to act with you.

That way, when you try to use the show as a launch pad for a mainstream commission, literary departments can say they "don't see evidence of an ability to write to scale".

That way, well-meaning people don't have to look at the fact that they are complicit in systematic discrimination. Those lessons are for other people to learn, in the community centres, in the regions up north, the Brexit voters and the Daily Mail readers.

Good people who work at the heart of the arts industry and spend their weekends running marathons for charity? Nah, they don't need to look at their behaviour. They are good, open people already. They meditate.

And do yoga.

Lots of yoga.

How could good people ever contribute to discrimination and oppression? That was never anyone's intention.

4

Scrounger is as true a story as you could put onstage in ninety minutes about an event that took over a year out of my life and ended with my signing a NDA regarding settlement. All of the true events are in the public domain. In October 2015 I was on a flight from London to Glasgow when I was removed from an aircraft as a result of my disability. When my £30,000 wheelchair was returned to me, it was severely damaged.

That alone would be a major traumatic event in anyone's life. But here's the thing: since October 2015, systematic discrimination has led me to drop out of an MA programme in creative writing, file a sexual misconduct claim at work, be verbally assaulted by another flight attendant on a different trip, lose friends who are unwilling to reflect on their actions, lodge two more discrimination lawsuits, and spend so much energy swallowing back the actions of good intentioned strangers, cabbies, shopkeepers, and professional colleagues because it's not worth it to point out their actions are wrong yet again.

As I write this, I have been unable to live in my home for two months, the result of an ongoing broken lift. Rather than replacing the lift, the building's management company keeps "hoping it will be sorted now".

This is the reality of living with a disability in 2019. It is constant, it is unending, and the things that do the most harm are the multitude of times well-meaning people get it very wrong, only to become upset when you try to call them out on their behaviour. Most people on the outside think systematic discrimination comes in the form of 'events'; big explosions which flare up on occasion, and then ultimately hibernate again for years. But the fact is, when people you love prove themselves complicit and even unwilling to challenge the very forces holding you back, it isn't an event; like sandpaper, it's a continuous erosion to your soul.

And so, in the middle of most trials, I have come to expect someone to say, "Hey, this would make a great one-woman show". I smile and agree because I've learned that this is easier than to ask most people to help me change the system. They are good people. They even believe in my artistic ability to put language to trauma. I just better not look at the system too closely. Not only might I show how the system favours well-meaning people, I might catch someone I care about being a cog in a system that depends on complicity in order to perpetuate itself.

Better to struggle to find the words, be onstage alone, a voice speaking into a near empty auditorium, regardless of whether anyone hears.

I sat down to write *Scrounger* as a one person show, but it became clear very quickly that a solo show was not the form this play needed to take. People fuck up this world again and again, especially those of us who take our pride from being non-confrontational, at the cost of making progress actually happen. One person alone railing against the injustices of the world onstage very quickly turns into navel gazing. From there, it's a very short step to thinking you're going to save children in Syria by running a marathon.

I'm not any more right, or liberal, or enlightened than anyone else out there. But the thing is, no one else gets to boast that either. Each of us manage to hurt those around us without ever really meaning to. But the second we put our value into being a good person and refuse to see how our actions can work in dead opposite to our intentions, we become someone's oppressor somewhere, even if the only people we are holding back are ourselves. Someone somewhere said 'The only thing necessary for the triumph of evil is for good men to do nothing', I disagree. I've come to learn that the triumph of evil can be helped along greatly by good people assuming they are doing a good job.

The fact is, stories are held together by conflict and confrontation. I could write a play about almost every day of my life because, when you live in the body that I do, avoiding conflict is not an option. The problem comes in when the people you love, expect you to avoid conflict simply because they themselves have always had the privilege of doing so.

That expectation is, by its very definition, oppression.

Scrounger was first performed as a staged reading as part of *Vibrant 2019 – A Festival of Finborough Playwrights* at the Finborough Theatre, London (Artistic Director: Neil McPherson) on Monday, 1 July 2019.

The cast was as follows:

Scrounger	Athena Stevens
P.A.	Tim Bowie

Directed by Georgie Staight

Scrounger received its world premiere at the Finborough Theatre, London (Artistic Director: Neil McPherson) on Tuesday, 7 January 2020.

The cast was as follows:

Scrounger	Athena Stevens
P.A.	Leigh Quinn

Directed by Lily McLeish
Designed by Anna Reid
Lighting by Anthony Doran
Sound by Julian Starr
Produced by Sarah Lawrie

Characters

SCROUNGER

P.A.

Here. Now.

SCROUNGER walks onstage from the back. Looking almost like she does not belong she wears trainers, a hoodie, leggings. She walks with an uneven gait, special, unique to her and her condition. There is something animal-like in the way her feet slap the floor, the gait of a mythical creature who, despite all the tension in her body, can still fall over if someone breathes the wrong way. She is relentless. Oblivion is not an option.

SCROUNGER stops a little too close for comfort. Seriously, who even let her on?

She talks directly to us, calling the audience out from moment one.

Yeah. I see you.

You think you like me.

You think it's brave that I am up here,

With my mouth forming strange shapes which somehow makes sounds,

Strung together that you're amazed you can understand,

Given two or three minutes.

You've already made up your mind that you will go home

Have a glass of Pimms with like-minded friends

And talk about how you sat through a borderline freak show... that you enjoyed!

Because that's how delightfully progressive you are.

Enlightened.

Left leaning.

Guardian reading, Daily Mail hating, Oxfam giving, colour blind seeing, red voting, paper straw using, conflict avoiding, zen loving, feminist supporting, always for the few… liberal minded you.

You'll say how it was hard to watch me, but you stuck through the awkward moments,

Because that's what a good open minded person does.

And you are a good person.

Waiting for some poor outsider like me, to be a vibrator to your ego.

See, I can say shit like that. Cuz you wanna like me.

> *SCROUNGER zeros in on our plant in the audience. This is the 'PA' who will play all of the other roles and do all of the actions to her. The PA can be played by any abled bodied person who is up to the job. Any race, gender, age etc.*

> *She gets right up in the PA's face. Licks it. Talks to the PA directly.*

What are you gonna do about it?

Huh?

> *SCROUNGER gets in between the PA's legs. This had better be part of the script. Then SCROUNGER addresses the whole audience.*

What are any of you gonna do about it?

> *The PA is jerked on the stage.*

Don't worry. I've done this before. Loads of times.

Haven't you?

> *The PA takes a second to adjust to being onstage, before grabbing SCROUNGER. The two actors together move like a choreographed dance, so there is no doubt that both actors are in it completely. Everything's fine folks…*

PA: Welcome to British Airways flight 8720 flying nonstop from London City Airport to Glasgow and served by BA City Flyer. Friends as you are aware we were supposed to leave twenty three minutes ago but we've had some technical hold ups. The good news is the wind is working in our favour, so we should be able to make up at least some of that time. We are just loading up the last few things into the hold now. Hopefully we'll be in the air by 7:30. Sit tight and remember: To fly. To serve.

6:55 AM flight out of London City Airport.

Made it out here by myself on the DLR,

That bit of TFL nobody really thinks about until they need it.

Then they go 'well this is nice. Thank God it's here!'

Truth is even though it's Monday morning,

I didn't even bother hitting the pillow last night.

Boyfriend and I just settled into a new flat in Elephant and Castle

And we had a few mates over to celebrate.

Emma's fiancee's just come back from filming in Syria,

And she wanted to talk about it.

The PA takes on the persona of Emma.

PA: Tom was fine. The company knew where they needed to stay and all that. But a tiny minority of people are keeping the majority oppressed. Children are being tortured. Children! And the hope of the Arab Spring is just gone! Asaad is crazy, Obama's doing fuck all. And I'm gonna run a marathon to do something about it.

Oh, well done Emma.

Do you want to do it with me?

Tell you what. As soon as you set up your JustGiving Page,

I'll be the first one to donate.

*PA takes on the role of Boyfriend. He slings a caring arm around
SCROUNGER as if to get Emma out of a scrape she's utterly unaware
she's in.*

**PA: I'll help you train, Em. About all she's good at on the
road is being a pace car in her wheelchair to be fair.**

*They kiss and then Boyfriend picks up a plate and heads back over
to Emma.*

PA: More kale chips and hummus Emma?

That's him.

The Boyfriend. He's done six marathons for charity.

Six.

That's 157.2 miles.

Another one and he'll have run the distance between London
and Manchester.

Helping strangers he doesn't even know.

Puts me to shame really.

PA switches back to Emma.

**PA: Great flat guys. Really. Have to say I wasn't that
thrilled when I saw the address. You know how I feel
about what LendLease did to the people who were
here.**

Here we go.

PA: BUT… I just want to say I really truly hope you both will be very happy here. I think you will be. So, hatchet is buried. Here's to the BEST couple south of the river.

Say what you want about gentrification and

What those property developers did to the people on the Heygate Estate was shit.

Utter shit.

I'd never do a thing like that if I was in charge.

But a new build means I can get in, lowered sinks in the kitchen,

Flat level showers, the wiring for a stair lift already built in,

Just in case I ever need it.

Boyfriend swears I won't,

That he'll keep me strong,

We'll do yoga and stretch every morning to make sure it's on the up from now on.

He always talks about how he wants to be like Gandhi

Change the world and make it as it should be.

So the yoga fits right in. Not that we were doing yoga this morning.

Although… Some people could call it that.

PA: Ladies and Gents I am so sorry, but it seems we had another hiccup in loading some last minute items. It'll be just another few minutes before we get going.

And everyone's kicking off.

Shocker.

I don't like to make a fuss.

What? No. I really don't…

The way I see it,

Everyone on this plane is about to fly.

Fly. In the clouds, just as the cool October sun is breaking over the horizon,

And get to Scotland early enough to do whatever we gotta do today,

Before flying back in ten hours to sleep in our own beds.

Most people onboard do it two or three times a week.

So I'm feeling all grown up and business-y.

> *SCROUNGER takes a camera out of her rucksack, shows it to us before checking to see if anyone onboard minds.*

University of Glasgow. I'm headed up to record an interview with Lee Cronin.

He's a Regent Professor there,

Started the world's first ever program in inorganic biology.

Don't worry I don't know shit about science.

But I have a YouTube channel where I–

PA: Excuse me Miss… Scrounger?

Yo??? Yes. What's up?

We are having some difficulties loading your wheelchair in the belly of the plane.

Do you want me to help you?

No. Not at all. It's quite a bit bigger than we were expecting.

I called ahead.

What?

The British Airways website said if you're flying out of London City

You need to call ahead with the measurements of–

You called ahead?

Yes. Two weeks ago.

OK. Um... Well we just thought you would like to know what the delay is. I'm sure we'll figure out something down below. 'To fly. To serve.' And all that.

Great.

Thanks.

It's a forced smile, lasting a bit too long as the PA leaves.

YouTube channel!

I've got over a quarter million subscribers,

Took my iPhone one day and asked a mate

How she defined success after she won a Paralympic Gold.

Posted it online for a lark, and lots of people said they wanted more.

That my questions were exactly what they needed,

The answers they wanted to hear on their dark nights,

So I set up a channel.

Boyfriend says that I make the world better.

I think,

No matter who we are and what we have to face,

This world is moving towards progress.

We only have to keep pushing long enough.

PA: Ladies and gents. I can only apologise again for the added delay. It seems that there is a passenger with a very large wheelchair onboard, much larger than we were prepared for. And we are having difficulty getting it into the hold. So if you're wondering why we haven't pulled away from the gate yet... there you go.

Well now I just feel fat.

PA: So if you could just hang tight for a few more minutes, we're going to resolve the problem shortly.

People start looking up and down the aisle,

Seeing if they can spot who exactly it is to blame.

PA: Sorry Miss...

Scrounger. Yeah. What?

PA: We're going to have to remove you from the flight. We are unable to get your wheelchair in the hold of the plane and I'm guessing you don't want to fly to Glasgow without it.

But I called ahead.

PA: We also can't figure out how to move your wheelchair.

I told you there's a release break–

**So we've been asked to escort you to the tarmac so you
can move it.**

What?

**PA: We need to get the plane away from the gate as
quickly as possible since we are now, really very
delayed.**

OK, but I don't need an aisle chair.

I walked onboard.

**PA: With the passengers waiting, we have been told to
get you off as quickly and safely as possible.**

The PA approaches lugging an airline aisle chair in tow.

*The PA clears away all seatbelts and the expectation is that
SCROUNGER will simply oblige.*

After a moment, she does. She tries to pull something out of her bag.

**PA: For those of you who don't know, and are now
sitting in a theatre feeling like it would be rude to
Google it, imagine half a chair sliced down the middle,
with eight sets of safety belts, and two small wheels in
the back so a person can only be rolled backwards and
Supine. Basically if Queen Cerci was in a wheelchair,
they'd make her do the walk of shame in an airline
aisle seat with a good chunk of her arse hanging out
either side.   Please sit back.**

I need to tell the guy I'm filming I'm not gonna make –

**PA: Please sit back so I can strap you in. We don't want
to make these people any later than they already
are.**

*The PA puts on the lap belt. And then the belt around her shins.
And then a belt that goes from her right shoulder to her left hip and*

another crossing SCROUNGER's chest in the opposite direction. Both of the latter make it impossible for her to move her arms.

Do I have to wear goggles too?

PA: What?

I feel like I'm getting ready to be shot out of a cannon.

The PA starts to pull SCROUNGER away.

Wait! My bag.

Sorry! It's got my recording kit in it is all.

The PA grabs the rucksack, then starts pulling SCROUNGER backwards again. Somehow the PA gets her to one side of the auditorium and starts pulling her backward, past individual audience members. She talks to them as she goes.

Now they're looking. Now they have someone to blame.

The individual who made their morning run late.

Never mind they groaned when the taxi rang and said they were delayed by seven minutes,

Or they hit the snooze one time too many,

Stayed in the kitchen a bit longer to get into a passive aggressive spat about the recycling,

Prayed to their inner gods that the gate would stay open sixty seconds longer,

So that they could grab one more latte from Starbucks,

But now it's all on me.

Their eyes flick up and watch me as I'm pulled down the aisle.

Then flick back down when they find I'm looking back.

Yeah, that's right, I'm looking back.

You'd better believe it.

This is wrong. And I'm gonna tweet the hell out of it,

As soon as I can get to my phone again.

The PA pulls SCROUNGER to some remote corner of the theatre, puts down her bag and starts to walk away.

Hey, hey, HEY! You're not gonna actually leaves me like this?

I'm already composing a tweet in my head,

Counting off characters and picking out words

To get people retweeting,

Talking,

Make sure that this doesn't happen to anyone else.

Few tweets, an apology,

Bet they might even give me a voucher.

Pause.

PA comes back on as a different airport worker. This individual speaks with an Eastern European accent.

Hiya, I'm waiting for my–

PA: I know. Yes? Wheelchair?

The PA takes the breaks off and starts to roll SCROUNGER backwards again.

OK, I hope you know where you're–

The PA puts on a pair of absurd ear blockers. SCROUNGER doesn't get a pair. The PA then gets not one but two electric hair dryers and a long orange extension cable, plugs both in, leaving her utterly baffled for a moment. Then the hairdryers are turned on, and blown directly into her face while at the same time the lights change and more sounds of the airport tarmac comes through.

PA: Can you hear me? Yes? It's there! It's there!

A siren is added to the noise as a damaged wheelchair is revealed. This thing isn't going to be gotten into during the production, but it is up to the design team to figure out how to illustrate the damage… The point is, it's fucked!

Upon the reveal, SCROUNGER who has thus far stayed admirably calm, starts to fight the restraints of the aisle chair to get out. The restraints stay firm as she fights. The PA runs over and starts to undo them but it's taking time.

Let me out!

PA: OK. OK. Calm down! I help you.

Now! Get it off!

PA: You OK. Calm down! I help!

Let me go! Get off.

PA: Miss. No! It not safe.

As soon as she can, SCROUNGER jumps out of the aisle chair and flees to her wheelchair.

The PA and hair dryers disappear.

The tarmac sound cuts out as the overwhelming alarm turns into a pathetic beeping coming from the chair itself. The rest is a cold silence.

She reaches over and pushes a button on the wheelchair's panel. The beeping stops.

I ask to be brought to the British Airways help desk,

We put the chair on the back of the buggy to get it there.

I nearly lose my balance climbing in shotgun.

Retracing where I've been already this morning,

The walls seem bigger,

Like Alice I've drunk the wrong potion and the world,

Which was almost alright an hour ago,

Is an opportunity for a nonstop assault.

Pay attention.

Get things right,

Don't leave out any details.

Tweet about it when you get home.

I start looking at everyone's name tags,

Making eye contact and noting who did what

So I can present my case with some sort of accountability,

Validity,

Credibility.

So I don't look like some kind of benefit scrounger out to get vouchers.

I didn't see the name tag of the first person,

The one that got me off the plane.

But this one I'm with now is named Ori,

And that one we are passing is... Emmanuel.

I look up for a CCTV camera to make sure it's getting us.

Ori, Emmanuel... Hector... Agnes.

A woman at the BA desk named Charlene offers

To have British Airways pay for an uber home.

The PA moves the two chairs in front of the wreckage to form a car, then helps SCROUNGER into the car, while passing her a piece of paper.

PA: Call this number when you get home, I've written my name here. We'll get you sorted out in no time love, all right? In the meantime, try to relax on the way home.

Ori, Emmanuel, Hector, Agnes, Charlene...

It'll work out.

I try to remind myself that this is how change happens.

The next few days might be rough, but after that,

It won't happen to anyone else.

Not at this airport at least.

Ori, Emmanuel, Hector, Agnes, Charlene...

I want the ride home to be quiet

But the driver turns on LBC

The PA produces a tape player, hits play and a fake LBC broadcast sounds with the voice of the PA. The player is placed in SCROUNGER's direction.

There is no level of hell

Which cannot sink further

With the addition of an LBC broadcast.

Next the PA takes out a mobile and calls her phone. If SCROUNGER cannot get it out of her rucksack the PA will ring again then get up, retrieve the phone and hand it to her. This takes however much time as it needs.

Shit! Professor Corrin!

Hi.

No, I'm not close.

It's a funny story as the airline-

I'm so sorry. I would like to reschedule if-

I see. Of course. Some other time then.

Hangs up. After a second she twists backwards to look at the wreck behind. The PA turns down the volume.

The driver tells me to SMILE.

On the word 'smile' the PA does full on jazz hands and says the word with or just after she does. It's the campest thing ever.

One look at his Nigerian flag

Hanging from the rearview mirror

I know it's not worth it to argue.

Right now I just want to get home

To Boyfriend.

To my laptop.

To set up my camera.

To do what needs to be done to get this right.

Then I'll smile.

But not before that mate.

PA: You know in my country–

Scrounger breaks form, lunges at the PA.

No. I'll say it! It's so bad, it'll just look racist if it comes from you.

He says where he comes from,

Children like me are thought to be from the devil,

Sent to torment their mums,

Like all evil spirits.

The PA makes some sort of pathetic 'spooky' noise.

Not today mate.

The PA looks back at SCROUNGER, expecting an answer. She responds.

We listen to LBC for the rest of the way.

Both jump out of their seats. The PA removes the chairs.

At home Boyfriend runs out to meet me in the car

Thankful that he is working from home today

Cuz God knows what would happen

If I had to get this inside, just me.

We are inside SCROUNGER's home with Boyfriend. Lights shift as if we are in an operating room examining the patient. If needed, Boyfriend might bring something over to allow SCROUNGER to sit so she isn't on the floor. She is drafting a tweet.

PA: What the fuck did they do?

They must have forced something somehow,

I haven't even begun to figure it out.

PA: Tyres are low?

26

That's the big problem, you think?

PA: I'm just saying they are.

But they were low before.

I was nagging you to get them pumped, remember?

PA: You don't need to be arsey about it.

I'm not. I'm –

Sorry.

Today started yesterday morning.

The PA looks at her, then reaches for an Allen key.

Did you get any sleep after I left?

PA: Emma called at seven. Wanted to start training Right. Now.

Of course she did.

Tightening that bit isn't gonna do much.

I mean it needs to be done, but as soon as you turn it on–

The PA hits the power button for the chair. The pathetic alarm starts up again.

PA: That's a noise I've never heard it make.

It won't drive,

That's the biggest problem.

If I can't get anywhere then–

PA: Get that phone call made and the tweet out. There's no use panicking when we don't know the full lay of the land.

You're right.

Boyfriend is right.

And I remind myself that this is why I like Boyfriend.

A consistent belief that this world can be made better,

That I am the type of person who can change it,

That's a good portion of the fire needed to start a revolution.

And it can start right now.

She takes out Charlene's slip of paper and dials. The PA produces another tape recorder. A prerecorded message starts up, complete with cheesy hold music.

PA: Hello.

Hiya–

PA: Welcome to British Airways Customer Service. Your call is very important to us. Please stay on the line.

OK, so…

The revolution starts once I'm done being on hold.

A passage of time and we see SCROUNGER and Boyfriend in a new position still working. Boyfriend has opened up the inner workings of the wheelchair.

PA: Welcome to British Airways Customer Service. Your call is very important to us. Please stay on the line.

Ori, Emmanuel, Hector, Agnes, Charlene…

Ori, Emmanuel, Hector, Agnes, Charlene…

Time passes again. Boyfriend still working but SCROUNGER has lost the will to live.

PA: Welcome to British Airways Customer Service. Your call is very important to us. Please stay on the line.

Boyfriend has now recruited SCROUNGER to be his "assistant". Both are fully committed to working together.

PA: Wire cutters.

Wire cutters.

PA: Clamps.

Clamps.

PA: Wipe my brow would you nurse?

Fuck no.

PA: Huh?

We're in a production at The Finborough. This isn't Holby City.

PA: OK. OK. I think I've sorted something.

PA: Welcome to British Airways Customer Service. Your call is very important to us. Please stay on the line.

WE KNOW!!!

The PA backs away from the innards of SCROUNGER's chair and presses the power button. The front lights start flashing, making us all crestfallen.

They need to fix it anyway.

PA: Knowing how these corporates work, they'll just blame us for–

The PA freezes, like a glitch before clicking into a different character. They are suddenly 100% not in the same presence as SCROUNGER.

PA: Thank You for holding. This is the British Airways Customer Service number, my name is Freddie, how can I help you today?

Hi. Hi. Hi. Hi. Hi. Hi!

PA: Hello.

Hi. I was flying out of London City Airport this morning,

Only I didn't fly out,

I was removed from the flight

And when my wheelchair was returned to me, it was severely damaged,

As in right now it won't turn on.

>   *Silence.*

I spoke to a woman named Charlene who said

If I rang this number,

You'd find her report filed and you could help me?

>   *Silence.*

>   *Both fall out of the moment in another time jump. When we see them again Scrounger is still on the phone and is clearly on a 'new tactic.'*

Eighteen minutes later Freddie has spoken to a supervisor.

Nobody has a clue what I'm talking about,

Or who Charlene is.

Ori, Emmanuel, Hector, Agnes, Charlene…

No matter, Boyfriend has a new tactic.

PA: One hundred forty characters. Just keep talking about it.

OK but why does London City Airport's handle have to be so long?

I don't even know who's at fault.

Them,

Or BA.

PA: So tag them both until you know.

Yeah but that cuts down on my character count by a quarter.

@British_Airways @LondonCityAir

That's 32 characters out of 140.

Gandhi never had this problem.

By the time we get to bed that night

My tweets have in total

13 likes

And 3 retweets.

Which isn't exactly the foundation for a revolution,

PA: Tomorrow I'll set you up to make a video. You missed a really big interview. That'll get people going. A quarter million subscribers right?

Right. There's a lot of power there.

The PA turns out the lights.

That night I go in and out of sleep.

You'd think being on none from the night before,

And what happened on the tarmac,

I'd be out for the count in full.

But I wake up in fits and starts,

Keep wondering

'What am I so worried about?'

And then I remember, I'm not going anywhere for a while.

My chair cost thirty grand.

They stopped making them three years ago,

The company went bust,

I can't just go out to Tescos and buy a new one.

We chose this flat based on what my chair can do,

As big as the airport seemed a few hours ago,

Our new flat seems just as small, the newness wearing thin.

By five thirty I know it's pointless to try and sleep any more.

So I make my way into the front room,

Thankful that I can walk on my own at home,

Sit on the couch and look out the window.

Our flat overlooks a park,

Still one place in Elephant and Castle where gentrification hasn't hit.

The building's WhatsApp group complains about

Men who sit outside and drink in the afternoon,

Congregating like pigeons giving their own commentary,

Whether the rest of us want to hear it or not.

But in the early morning hours they are not there.

Just a few folks walking their dogs.

Lights change fast, PA brings on a camera and sets up to record.

By nine AM I've sent out thirty tweets.

To papers,

And reporters,

And the mayor,

And Labour,

And Conservaties,

AND STEPHEN FRY. Just to see if I can get his attention.

I have seven retweets.

If a picture is worth a thousand words,

Think of what a YouTube video can do.

> *SCROUNGER points to the PA and the camera starts recording. We see the image projected onto the back wall of the stage. Presenting on YouTube is completely natural for her.*

So now I'm here. In my flat. For who knows how long. I'm trying not to think of the worst case scenario. It won't come to that. But I'm a bit stuck as to who to turn to next. So if any of you have any ideas… that'd be great. Oh, and retweet this video tagging @British_Airways @LondonCityAir. Thanks! Bye!

> *The PA stops recording.*

PA: It's less than thirty six hours from the event. It's still going to be fine. This is all just a misunderstanding. Once you talk to the right person, in the right office, And explain exactly what happened, you can fix it.

This is how the world changes,

If I can get this right,

I can change the world.

Her phone ring and she answers.

Hey Emma.

PA: It's like you're fucking Martin Luther King!

Why do you sound like your running?

PA: I'm training! For the kids in Serbia.

Syria?

PA: Right, them. But your video. It's brilliant. Clear, concise, funny, charming. How you were able to explain the situation in under six fucking minutes is beyond me. And I've retweeted it, so that is something.

Thanks for that Em. Hopefully it'll get–

PA: Girl, you know I love it when you get political! Be the change. We need you.

That's good to hear.

PA: And the best part is, the longer you are without a chair, the longer you're just stuck at home, able to tweet whatever you want. Good luck with that mate.

Wish I had your confidence,

PA: Nah, come on... this is... this is...

Are you ok Em?

Maybe you shouldn't run and talk to me,

At the same time,

At least not yet.

Emma stops running.

34

PA: Probably. It's just the kids probably go through way worse, fleeing Asaad or whoever, you know? I can barely run 5K. Anyway... Right... Just keep doing what you are sooner or later it will get a reaction. Yeah?

Yeah.

PA: Cool. Hey, do you want to meet me in town for a drink later? I could really use a pint after this run.

A reaction from SCROUNGER to us. WTF is Emma even on about?

Ummm, Emma?

PA: What?... Oh right! Sorry, wasn't thinking.

You could come over here.

PA: Nah, I don't really want to leave the centre of town.

Elephant and Castle is Zone 1.

PA: Yeah, I know they say that but... is it really?

She hangs up.

Twenty Three retweets of my video by dinner.

My interviews usually get more traction by now.

But it's a weird one,

Asking for help when my brand is usually being "unstoppable."

When Boyfriend comes home I sit on the couch,

Watching him as he tries to keep the eggs in the pan from catching.

Look out our window and see people on their way back from work,

Cutting through the park with laptop bags slung across their shoulders,

Avoiding eye contact with those blokes drinking on the bench.

In the middle of all of them, three teenage girls pass through,

Looking all alike in their grey school uniforms.

The one in the middle, wears a head scarf and pushes herself in a wheelchair.

I can tell

Even from looking across the park and six stories up,

She is stronger than people in her life give her credit for.

I mean, physically stronger.

She rolls along the pavement at the same rate as her friends,

Laughing and pointing at one of the other girls as she makes a complete fool of herself.

Her chair is NHS standard,

They're shit.

But hey, it's the NHS, you're disabled, and they're free,

So you learn to be grateful right?

I call Boyfriend over and he puts the pan down,

Stands by the sofa while I point out the trio.

"She pushes herself, despite having those stupid push handles in the back of her chair."

PA: So?

"High back chairs like that are miserable to push,

36

You keep slamming your elbows into the handles every time you sling your arms back.

The chair is meant to be built for you,

But there's these two handles in the back that get in your way,

Every time you try to move.

They are back there, to make it easier,

For everyone else, to manipulate you.

Get it?"

Three weeks go by.

I've written over four hundred tweets tagging @british_airways

And @LondonCityair.

The best they can do?

PA: Under the Montreal Convention, airlines are not held liable for damages to personal effects over £1,200.

Even though they broke it themselves.

I haven't been outside the entire time.

PA: On the plus side, you've edited that backlog of interviews you had to finish. So that's something.

Online retweets are holding steady with about twenty or thirty per day.

Some of the comments remind me I'm not alone.

> *The PA switches characters between each line, the details of who the characters are is up to the production.*

PA: Capitalist pigs! Really @British_Airways should pay more attention to people and not turning a profit.

PA: OMG! This poor girl can't get anywhere cuz her wheelchair has been smashed up by the airline, and nobody's doing anything! WTF is wrong w ppl?

PA: This exact thing happened to my nan last year when we took a family trip to Disney. Whole family holiday ruined. Never got it sorted.

Some comments try to be helpful.

PA: Did you try turning it off and turning it back on Love? Always works with my computer.

Of course! Why didn't we think of that?

PA: We've got a chair we could loan you in the garage. It's my spare for when we travel so shit like this doesn't happen. It's not electric, so someone will have to push you. But it's something.

If only wheelchairs were interchangeable.

And probably about every three days or so,

I get one of these.

PA: Oh look, another lazy scrounger trying to get what she can off of benefits, while the rest of us work. You delayed an entire flight of people AND you want a new chair? Get real mate.

PA: Classic benefit scrounger, right here.

PA: Get a job and buy yourself a wheelchair. (And no, videos on YouTube don't count as a real job. Soz)

PA: Spastic.

Actually, I'm not spastic, I'm athetoid.

PA: Spastic.

Well, scientifically speaking you are incorrect–

PA: Spastic.

I'm the opposite of that actually, because

Spastic is when you have really really tight muscles.

And when I was born, I was what was known as a floppy baby.

So I'm not actually spastic I'm the dead opposite see?

PA: Well, I've never heard of that. Must be a fake diagnosis.

Yeah, alright mate. You caught me.

SCROUNGER gives us a scathing look.

PA returns to Boyfriend.

PA: God, the idiocy of some people! They don't have a leg to stand on. You do know that right?

Are you sure you don't want to use a different metaphor here?

PA: I mean legally… The airport, or airline, I haven't figured out which

And they can't figure it out either.

PA: Well one of them is about to have a really big problem on their hands, because *legally… legally* I've been doing some Googling at work, and there's this EU law. EU Law 1107/2006 it's called. I think it's your trick to getting some legal action.

PA pulls out phone.

In addition to creating a Twitter Storm,

We've been looking for a law,

Something to point to absolutely,

As a fact that smashing up my chair was objectively wrong,

And the airline and airport can point fingers all they want,

But someone, somewhere is going to have to pay up,

Right

Fucking

Now.

We've been looking for this, we haven't had much luck.

PA: Turns out this EU Regulation says, well first of all it says that once you are on the flight, you can't be gotten off, due to reasons of your disability, so... DING... that's the first fuck up there... secondly, the flight that you were on specifically had a door that was too small to fit electric wheelchairs. They had no business letting you keep that ticket when you called ahead, so DING... that's the second fuck up there. And finally, if they do break your wheelchair, the airport is required – now this is huge- they are required to provide you a replacement chair? Ummm... do you see a replacement anywhere in this flat?

Ummm... no!

Umm... I don't either. Make a video, send a tweet, scare the living shit out of them, cuz this warrior princess isn't going down without a fight!

They embrace. Nothing but clear skies ahead.

I knew there was a law, or a regulation, or something,

There had to be something.

Something on paper, something other than guilt.

Something other than the names I keep repeating to myself,

Ori, Emmanuel, Hector, Agnes, Charlene,

While praying that CCTV cameras were on,

To hold people to account.

Something that said, 'This is wrong,

And other people see it too.'

SCROUNGER's phone rings, she lets go of the PA to answer.

Hey Emma, how are ya?

PA: God, you sound great. Did you get news about your chair?

Not yet. But we've got a plan,

PA: That's such good news. Listen, I can't come tonight. I think I must have twisted something when I was out training. Tom's worried that the walk from the station might do me in. And I have to run for these kids in Siberia. I can't let them down.

Syria. Don't they get the money even if you don't run?

PA: I don't know. That's a good question. Anyway it sounds like you'll be back out and about in no time, so maybe we can meet in town like next week.

My flat is in town.

PA: Alright. I know some people would call it that. Anyway, I'll see you soon yeah. Lots of love. Bye.

Ever noticed there's a type of woman in the UK,

That when she says 'lots of love, bye,'

Her voice goes up like she's not sure she means it?

PA answers in their own voice.

PA: uhhh... no?

Just me then.

EU 1107/2006 seems to be written with exactly my case in mind.

When chairs are smashed up beyond repair,

And nobody wants take responsibility for it.

The regulation holds airports responsible

For making sure the passenger affected isn't

Stranded without some sort of wheelchair if what happens did,

And airlines are responsible if the chair is damaged inside the cargo hold.

There's nothing about if the chair gets stuck in the doorframe of the plane.

But we'll get there.

That's what makes the law so interesting.

Right?

Boyfriend and I decide that this can now be a three pronged attack.

He is on board with the first two,

But with the third, he says, I'm totally on my own.

PA: First, you keep tweeting. And making videos. We are going to start quoting EU1107/2006 back to them, remind them of their obligations. And we are going to add the hashtag 'dayswithoutawheelchair'. The

**clock is ticking and every time the sun sets, they
screw themselves a little bit more.**

There's not been much going on in response to me online,

Their social media teams seem to be set to ignore,

Like if it takes long enough, I'll just go away.

But maybe some added accountability will change that.

We figure out it will be 35 days tomorrow since this
happened.

35 days without mobility,

35 days not leaving the flat,

35 days without sunshine,

35 days without filming interviews,

35 days without meetings,

Coffee,

Going to the Shops,

All of it.

Didn't occur to me it was that long.

The PA tries to get SCROUNGER out of her vortex.

**PA: Number two… Number two is that I'm going to
reach out to this guy who runs this website. He offers
assistance in getting people what they have a right
to in these situations. Let's meet him and see if he's
willing to help us.**

I look out the window, six stories down

The teenager from before pushes her chair though the park,

Some shopping hanging on the back handlebars.

I'm glad she's found a use for them.

After a second the bag slides off,

Her elbow, going back for a push, knocks it

Off the handle and onto the ground.

One of the men, drinking on the bench offers help,

And within a moment she is back on her way again.

Isn't it amazing,

How people can take action,

When they really, really want to?

SCROUNGER turns to PA.

Number three.

PA: Number three?

Yeah, I'm going to call a lawyer, a solicitor, a regulator,

Whatever the fuck the right person is,

And see if I can start taking legal action.

PA: Woah now, hang on.

Yeah?

PA: That's not in the script.

Say what now?

PA: That wasn't on my list.

Well, it's on mine.

It has to be.

Pause.

There's no point in fighting back

If the law doesn't work in our favour.

PA: We can't regulate everything. If you just take your time and explain things properly, clearly in your videos, without looking like a victim, I'm sure–

OK, what was your number three?

PA: It seems a little off point now... You can't...

What?

PA: It just seems a little front foot and aggressive is all.

AGGRESSIVE!!!

It's been 35 days,

I've been trying to engage online,

Reasonably.

This EU regulation shows they are clearly in the wrong.

It is reasonable. The law is REASONABLE.

PA: I know that sure. You've done great. Doing great. I just...

We seem to be off script here,

So you really need to finish that sentence for me.

PA: Aren't you afraid you're going to become known, just as the person that sues everyone?

No.

Just out of curiosity, what was your number three.

PA: Sex.

I don't think that should be on the table tonight,

Do you?

PA: Maybe not.

Look, I don't really want to talk to a solicitor either.

But it can't hurt to talk to someone,

Find out some answers, so that everyone knows,

When this happens to someone else again,

Where things stand.

It's just one step,

Right?

Boyfriend agrees to contact the guy who runs the website,

But I'm on my own to find a solicitor.

I look out my window for the teenager outside,

But she seems to be long gone.

I can't help but think of her as I fall asleep

Next to boyfriend.

It feels like that he is already,

Very far away.

Maybe if I go through this whole ordeal, get it right,

Play the hand, prove my case, bring out

Ori, Emmanuel, Hector, Agnes, Charlene,

As evidence,

Maybe she won't have to go through it too.

I turn to Boyfriend next to me in bed,

Just to make sure he's still there,

And not been replaced by some giant carrot or something.

I reach out and touch his back,

It's warm and and moves up and down with his steady, restful breath.

And there's a question stuck in my throat that somehow

Moves my tongue without much effort.

"You're on my side… right."

The PA lets out a giant man-snore.

Later.

Some days later.

Actually, no, why the fuck am I saying that?

I know exactly how long it's been.

We are on 47 hashtag days without a wheelchair.

Boyfriend has set up a meeting with the guy who runs the website.

I'm still stuck on Citizen's Advice chats asking all the stupid questions,

I can ask for free, before I have to plonk down any money,

To hire a solicitor. Maybe this guy will make it clear,

Exactly what we have to do next.

Maybe nobody can help.

The PA by this point has helped to get SCROUNGER into the car, and then goes into the driver's seat as the SAME Uber driver we've had twenty pages ago. SCROUNGER can't believe her luck.

You again?

PA: You know, in my country–

No, I've got this.

Boyfriend chats to the Nigerian driver the whole way there.

I used to love him for it,

How he could talk to anyone, put them at ease,

Bring out the best and make a connection.

But as I listen, I swallow hard to notice within myself,

I just can't be fucked

After 47 days.

And although boyfriend is sitting right next to me,

To hear him talk about it like it's just a blip,

A misunderstanding.

I'm starting to wonder if he gets it.

The driver looks back to both of us,

Boyfriend holding my hand as I look out the window.

It's my first time out since my mobility was taken away,

And everything feels overwhelming, too much, too bright,

We're going too fast,

Is this how fast cars normally go?

The driver tells me to smile more,

That I have so much to be joyful about if I only glance around to look.

Jazz hands:

Smile!

The guy who runs the website is named Mario,

Italian,

He kisses me on the cheek after he shakes boyfriend's hand.

I try to tell myself that it's cultural, that's all.

But I still feel the imprint of his beard on my face,

Long into the conversation.

Then I wonder how many times he's seen the Godfather.

PA: This seems to be a, as the English would call it, "clear violation" of the EU regulations. Even if her chair never got through the door of the airplane, the regulations state that there is a duty of care to this woman–

Hi, I'm right here, just so you know.

PA: Of course you are! I apologise. The point is the EU governing bodies would be more than interested to know that London City Airport has failed on several occasions in regards to your case, not the least of which as they provided you with no temporary replacement chair, at all. I don't know how the airport ever thought they would get away with that!

Are you sure? I mean with everybody needing something different–

PA: Of course, of course. Airports aren't going to have a wheelchair like yours sitting in some back room. Yours was a luxury model, a sports car-

Mine was what I needed. Prescribed to me by my doctor.

PA: As you say, but to provide no replacement at all... Leave it with me.

But what can you do?

PA: I am known in European circles as someone who is passionate about air travel for individuals such as yourself. I'm on my way to Brussels at the end of next month–

Next month?

PA: And can ask about your case directly with those in the know. Give it time as you say. The right thing always wins out in the end.

Makes to leave, then stops.

PA: Oh and, if I can say this selfishly... Keep making your videos. I mean the ones with the hashtag days without a wheelchair. For my own part, any light that can be shed on what's happening, not just to you, but across the industry, is a good thing in my book. We need it.

He might say the right things,

We might even both be on the same side,

I mean we are, we clearly are.

But the way he acts like this is open and shut,

Even after 47 days...

I don't want to go back inside when we get to the flat

SCROUNGER's mobile receives a notification.

But there's email waiting.

Two actually.

First one is from a solicitor, saying she's had a look,

At my questions and my timeline.

Would I like to have a chat?

No promisses.

No fees.

But there might be something,

We can do if we put our heads together.

The second,

The second is from 38 Degrees,

One of those online petitions forums,

Trying to get people together to change the world.

People in their office are on the hunt for bad situations,

Fights that need to be fought, which never should be fights to begin with.

They've seen my videos.

They've been following my Twitter feed.

They are disgusted there hasn't been any action yet.

Has there?

No. Nothing but shoving things under the rug from the people who need to fix it,

I met with a guy today who might be able to help,

In a few weeks.

But I'm still stuck without being able to get anywhere

And needing to get back to interviews like,

Now.

PA: Hiya… Yeah, so. we'd like to initiate a petition on you behalf to both parties. Just to let you know, we can't be held legally responsible for anything that might work against you. But it looks like what you need more than anything is media attention, and we can certainly get you that.

YES! YES! YES!

I might type at 13 words per minute,

But I write them back in a flash.

Yes I want to meet with a solicitor

A female solicitor and get her opinion on what actually might be done.

And yes, let's get a petition started,

As big as we can make it so that maybe,

Just maybe,

It'll click how wrong this is,

And airlines will take action to stop it.

Within hours both opportunities have been set up.

I'll meet the solicitor at the coffee shop round the corner from my flat.

I can get boyfriend to leave me there a few hours,

Just as an excuse to get out.

And the petition is up,

Online, with a selfie of me next to the damaged chair looking sad.

The blurb about what happened includes info about EU 1107

Just in case anyone wants to think that what happened was

A misunderstanding.

Four hours later there are

One hundred sixty nine signatures.

And my tweets are getting the biggest boost yet.

SCROUNGER squeals.

This is already way better than anything I've managed on my own.

People are amazing.

PA: I thought we decided this morning that Mario was going to help you.

And he said 'keep talking,'

So that's what we are doing,

PA: I don't want to piss anybody off is all. If he says–

Piss who off?

I've been pissed of for weeks,

Doesn't that count for anything?

PA: Pissed off at me?

No, of course not at you!

Just at the whole situation.

Don't you think I have a right to be angry,

After all of this?

PA: I understand that. You should be upset. But angry? You've got the law on your side and a man going all the way to Brussels for you. Let it work out. You don't have to take it all on yourself. This system might be slow, but it is there.

Then why does it keep happening?

PA: Let's just try and make the best of it, and not go off seeking an over emotional shit show

The 'best' will be if this never happens again.

To anyone ever. Not just me.

We're supposed to be making the world a better place,

Isn't this part of it?

Pause. The PA walks away.

Boyfriend doesn't say much for the rest of the night,

But in that time, during that brief conversation,

Thirty Three more people have signed the petition,

And I can feel something building,

About ready to break.

I decide to meet the solicitor at the flat,

When Boyfriend isn't in,

Just so he doesn't have to take me anywhere.

Sure, it means I miss my chance to go out,

But in the long run, I am trying to keep the conflict in my life

Down to a minimum, regardless of how it looks like to everyone else,

On the outside.

PA reenters as a female solicitor. Rings doorbell and settles in. She carries a Starbucks cup and presents it proudly to SCROUNGER.

PA: As requested.

Coffee.

Real coffee from the outside world.

Not granules or a paccachino,

The proper stuff from a real machine.

PA: Are you sure that's all you wanted? A Starbucks coffee seems a pretty low bar for happiness.

Thank you.

PA: You're welcome. It just doesn't seem like much for someone who hasn't been out of the house for weeks and weeks.

No, really. Thank you,

It's a lot.

PA: Yeah, I get it. OK, so… Well, I've had a look at EU 1107/2006 and the rest of the European Union air travel regulations. But, I hate to say it, nobody has put these regulations to the test. Everyone is skating around on a law that isn't really defined, and no one wants it to be. For example, I don't see anything about them _having_ to send you home with a wheelchair.

It says the airport has to provide an appropriate replacement.

PA: Yes, but for how long?

What?

PA: It says nothing about for how long. Is it for all of
time? I doubt it. Or is it just until they can roll you
outside the door of the airport and dump you at the
curb.

If there isn't a set limit, you have to wonder why?
I know what we want it to say, every Guardian
reading person who fancies themselves liberal
thinking wants it. But that's not what's written down.
The big wigs in the air travel industry are not into
moving people. They are into making profit. People
like you cut into their profit.

I've noticed.

PA: In fact, if this had to go to court, I'm not sure if I
would want to take it. I mean don't get me wrong,
you are clearly on the side of justice. That's the side
I want to be on, when I can. Problem is, the law isn't
on that side too. And it won't be, until the law gets
tested. Which means someone getting up the guts to
take it to court.

Which won't be you.

PA: No. But it could be you. I'm sorry. Enjoy your
coffee.

*The PA shakes SCROUNGER's hand and leaves. A message comes
in on her phone. SCROUNGER plays it, it's from Mario.*

PA: Hello my little Scrounger! Hope you are having
a day that's just *Marvillosa* – as we would say back
home. Listen I wanted to let you know that I just got
off the phone with a couple of the EU regulators,
the ones that were actually in the room back in 2006
when they wrote EU 1107. They know that regulation

and its intention backwards and forwards *and they insist,* they insist that the reg falls down on your side, and that it will do so when I present your case at the tribunal in a few weeks.

Meanwhile... five thousand people on that 38 Degrees petition. Well done little Scrounger for digging those up! I'm so impressed and begging you, please, keep it up! We need this story to get out and YOU... YOU ARE DOING IT.

The PA comes on using an iPhone as a recorder as well as snapping away with a flash camera. SCROUNGER poses with the chair as Mario's message keeps being played.

PA: Just keep talking. Keep up the momentum online and with any press they throw at you. In a few weeks time, I'll have the verdict everyone already knows is true.

PA starts speaking as a journalist.

PA: Can you tell me how it feels to not be able to get out day after day?

I really don't want feelings to enter into this, if I'm honest. I've had a lot of people say I'm overly emotional. This is wrong. It's wrong to take someone's mobility away and not engage or take responsibility for it. Full stop. No amount of me going on about how terrible it is will change that.

PA: So would you say you're frustrated by the people who are at fault?

If I knew who they were, I would be. The airline industry is set up so that loads of people can blame each other, but no one has to take responsibility. Now where in British society have we seen that before?

More flash bulbs.

The PA becomes another reporter.

PA: BBC Radio 1 news. Your online petition has been up for 3 weeks and has received over 24,000 signatures in that time. This is extraordinary. Have you seen any response from either British Airways or London City Airport?

No.

PA: At all? Frank Gardner, a reporter here at the BBC is also a wheelchair user and live tweeted yesterday about his treatment at Heathrow. Yet you are saying no engagement has occurred.

Mate, I'm still waiting for a refund for a flight I never got to take because I was removed from the aircraft as a direct result of my disability.

PA: There ought to be a law!

More flash bulbs. The PA changes to a Newsnight reporter with massively upbeat, racy music.

PA: Tonight we have a very special, special young woman who is taking on the giants of the sky. Her petition on 38 Degrees has garnered over 26 thousand signatures and shows no signs of slowing down. I was lucky enough... hang on... no... no... we can't say that. I wasn't 'lucky enough to catch up with her' because she's been stuck in her flat the past two months. Can we get some more appropriate music here? Violins would be nice.

So you don't want me to smile?

PA: Yes! No... Actually, I don't know? Do whatever you think is best and we'll go with it! An expression that really captures the complexity of the situation.

SCROUNGER looks at us, bewildered.

PA: There you go! Nice!

They say you wait for a bus,

And then three come along,

Which automatically makes you wonder if you

Got your messaging right in the first place.

I've seen the movies like Selma,

Hidden Figures... Gandhi...

All that shit has been and gone in the course of two hours.

Three if Ron Howard is directing it.

So I'm a storyteller,

It's my job to break this down into a straight trajectory,

That makes sense.

My job here is to create,

A story.

That shows progress is being made and people like me,

People who you think are people like you,

The fighters on the front covers of the papers you read,

Always win out.

That's my job, that's the storytellers job,

To tell a story so that you can come home,

And sleep easy.

But I'm going to tell you,

I'm going to tell you right fucking now,

Since this happened back in October 2015,

Before Brexit,

Before Johnson,

Before Grenfell,

Before Trump,

I have not had one good night's sleep without drugs.

The filmmakers always edit those dark nights out.

Those scenes get written and then they get dropped,

Cuz it makes the movie too long,

Or the focus group doesn't like it.

Did you know that?

Or does progress go in a straight line as far as your

Ideals are concerned?

> *A voicemail from Mario plays as the PA sets up a yoga mat and starts doing the most absurd yoga routines imaginable. To the point of it being a little bit distracting. SCROUNGER holds the phone trying to block Boyfriend out and hear what's going on.*

PA: Principesa! You're interview on SkyTV! Well done! You didn't tell me about that one. I can tell you're the type of girl I have to keep all eyes on. Well, what's a poor man like me to do? Listen I'm just packing for the big trip to Brussels, wondering how you are… minus not having your 'legs' of course. You had to get the most expensive model wheelchair and complicate everything for all of us huh?

**Listen, I wanted to say… and mind you, I'm not the
type of man who says this often… This case is really
helping me out professionally. Helping us all out I
mean. I have a son with CP, just like you, so when I
speak for you, I speak for him. What I am doing is
that important really.**

SCROUNGER speaks to Boyfriend.

Can you please stop oming for just a minute?

Boyfriend does.

**PA: I also wanted to just say, please do not worry about
the wording of the regulation. I know the council
in Brussels very well. They are reasonably minded,
thorough people. Very thorough. Which is more than
I can say about the British Civil Aviation Authority.
These English are so into the letter of the law, not the
spirit. I understand your concern, but let them melt
away like the sun melts the snow. In the European
Union, better heads will prevail. Ciao Bella.**

I don't trust him.

Well not 'him' that sounds a bit–

PA: Paranoid?

Boyfriend starts to go back to his yoga.

I wasn't going to say that.

If the regulation worked the way everyone thinks it should,

Why would it have even happened in the first place?

Her phone receives a text.

It's a producer,

Wanting to know if they can come by

61

Tomorrow morning and shoot for the breakfast show?

It's early,

Like really early.

PA: Go on.

Like 4 am early.

PA: Fuck no.

It's just me in the flat,

We can do it in the front room,

You can stay in bed the entire time.

PA: Nobody needs to be talking to a camera crew that early in the morning. Why can't you just let Mario sort it? Let everything take its course and it will be fine.

A very long, loud silence. SCROUNGER really doesn't want to spill the beans. Then, Boyfriend says in mid warrior pose.

PA: We should really get you up and doing something. I think it might help you relax some.

What if I waited outside the flat,

So you wouldn't even hear them ring the bell?

PA: Are you fucking kidding me? No. Alright? No. The revolution can wait until 8:30 AM at least. God, I honestly think– there's something about this entire circus that you downright enjoy. Let it go will you? Just for 24 hours can you let this thing go?

Boyfriend goes back to the warrior pose.

Boyfriend and I don't talk much for the rest of the night.

Later I see the teenage girl in the park down below,

Pushing her usual course on her way home,

There's no one in the park at that hour

So she pushes her chair alone.

The rhythm of her arms swinging back and forth where the pavement is flat

Slows dramatically as soon as she reaches the smallest incline.

Her hands fighting friction to move forwards

And then flinging back as quickly as possible,

So that no momentum is lost in between the pushes.

Most people would call it brave

Seeing that level of struggle,

Their arms couldn't handle it.

But it's just what you do,

When you have to,

Because life doesn't give you much of a choice,

But to move forward, even when so many people question,

Whether or not all that struggle

Is just arrogance fighting against where fate has put you all along.

Boyfriend and I sleep back to back

And when the phone lights up my side of the bed

With a text from the show-runner wanting confirmation,

I turn on Do Not Disturb and turn the phone facedown on the bed.

He is right,

There is part of me that likes being heard.

Which is why I'm so worried,

If Mario is wrong,

What will my voice be then?

And what will happen to that teenager outside.

SCROUNGER's phone rings. It's Emma.

The next morning.

PA: You are ABOVE THE FOLD ON THE GUARDIAN WEBSITE, WOMAN!

(To us)

It wasn't me!

The Guardian has been waiting three days to release my story.

Still, Boyfriend is not pleased.

(To Emma.)

You can't be above the fold on a website, Em.

PA: Whatever, I don't need to scroll down to see you. YOU'RE RIGHT THERE.

Give it a couple hours, that'll change.

How's training for the kids in Syria?

PA: So hard. Running is really hard work you know? I had no idea, did you?

Nope, none at all.

PA: I'm going to have to check in with your beau next week to see if he has any ideas. I don't think it's supposed to be this hard, frankly.

You're training for a MARATHON, Emma.

PA: I KNOW! And people do it all the time. All these charity runs are full of people who have never done it, so why am I finding it this hard?

SCROUNGER looks at us, about ready to chuck in the towel.

PA: Anyway, screw it. It's my birthday this weekend and even if I am training, a girl still has to have fun. Soooo, I was wondering.

Yeah.

PA: I was wondering if you were busy Saturday night?

Well, I'm not going out much right now am I?

PA: Huh? Oh, right, yeah. Sorry. Duh.

It's fine.

PA: Anyway, we are having some friends out to the top floor of the White Stag on Saturday for some drinks. If by some miracle you have a chair, you can leave it downstairs. Either way we can carry you up.

Carry me up?

PA: Sure. Tom will be on hand if the two of you can't manage. It's no big deal. And if anything you'll look like the queen of Sheba.

Em, why haven't you visited our flat

Since the day before the accident?

PA: I know, I know. If this goes on for much longer, I'll get there, eventually.

Eventually?

PA: Well, it hasn't really been this long when you think about it.

It was 76 hashtag days without a wheelchair today.

Not that you would notice, it's been pretty much all the same for you.

Did you know, this entire time,

Nobody has offered to get me out of the flat once.

You've been out running up and down the hills

Of Nappy Valley North London for the children

In some country whose name you can't even remember,

And you can't be bothered to figure out

If your best mate needs anything from Tescos,

Where have you been Emma? And then maybe you can tell me why

After all these years of being my friend,

You can't be fucked to plan your own piss up

In a location I can get into?

    Silence.

PA: If you're going to talk to me that way, you can just forget the entire invitation. You know, I've watched you on the news the past few weeks and I've even been quite proud. You want to change the world, that's great. God knows this world is one that has to

be changed. And you want to be political, fine. The best of us need to be political too. But do not even think of getting political around me.

You know who you ought to look at? Martin Luther King. Or Gandhi. Both of them managed to change the world without upsetting anybody. Aim to be like them, a peace maker.

I'm just gonna chalk this up to you being stressed. Maybe you'll cool down when everything is sorted.

Emma hangs up.

Sorted.

When is everything going to be sorted?

The way we are headed in this world,

Is it all ever gonna be sorted?

I used to think,

In school we would repeat this to each other,

That we were on the up.

That given enough time,

Working together in our lifetimes,

Humanity would hit equality, we just had to wait it out.

And I believed that.

But.

Now.

After 76 days of watching for an answer,

Waiting for someone to take action,

To get it,

To go beyond apologies and saying

The situation is 'unfortunate'

To fix a problem that is easily sorted,

A sure ticket bet home run for publicity and good PR,

I don't believe we are headed towards progress anymore.

I just can't.

People like Emma wanna look woke,

But still order room service,

Can't be bothered to put their feet on the ground to do,

Some fucking work.

And I don't know how to engage,

With people on the wrong side of justice,

That can't be bothered to tell their left

From what's right.

PA enters as boyfriend.

PA: Don't break things off with our friends.

Well where has she been for the past ten weeks?

PA: People get busy, we all have our lives out of–

The flat? Yes I know,

I used to have one too.

I would really like to get back to mine.

PA: Well you won't have any friends left if you keep shutting out the ones we have.

Why didn't you have her jog by

On one of her training routes?

It's four miles between here and Islington,

You'd think after two months of training her,

She'd be able to get that far.

PA: I don't want to get into it with you. You know me. I don't really like conflict.

Why are you saying that like it's a good thing?

PA: Because the last I checked, it was!

Look, I'm sorry… Just… would you please trust Mario. Trust that today we have a system in Europe that doesn't let shit like this happen without a fight. I don't like to see you fighting, when someone else can.

I met with a solicitor,

The regulations aren't clear,

We are relying on goodwill,

Which I'm not seeing very much of at this point.

We need to keep working and not wait–

PA: What do you mean you 'met with a solicitor.' You haven't been outside the flat for weeks.

She came here,

Brought me a coffee.

At least someone bothered to drop by.

PA: Why can't you trust–

We can't see what we want in a law,

What we think ought to be there when it clearly isn't.

I don't trust that everything is all right anymore,

More often than not,

It's going to take a fight.

PA: No. No, no, no, no, no, no. That's not how we do things. You need to stay positive. This is a result of taking too much on rather then just letting things become what they are. Tomorrow morning we will get up early and we'll salute the sun. We'll do some breathing exercises and some yoga. You'll feel much better after–

When have we ever done yoga?

PA: What?

We talk about doing yoga,

Doing what needs to be done to keep me strong,

To make the world a better place.

But when have we actually taken the time,

To do it, rather than just talk about 'someday'?

Pause.

Even in all this time,

When there was nowhere else to go,

Did we ever? Once?

PA: We'll start tomorrow.

No, we won't.

It'll be easier not to

And we will be more happy with the possibility that

We could be people who do that,

Than actually going forward and doing something.

**PA: Come on. There's a first step and it's always the
most difficult.**

I don't think it is.

I think the hardest step,

Is when you realise the people who you thought,

Would always have your back,

Haven't been there all along.

When they just tell you to smile more,

But can't actually be bothered to bring the issue to a head
themselves,

How do you fix a relationship after that?

When you're both basically living on different planets,

And can't imagine a visit once in a while?

The lease was in my name

And we chose the flat because of my needs so…

He had just carried out the last box

When I noticed a new voicemail on my phone.

SCROUNGER plays a recording from Mario.

PA: Hello, Bella. Listen I have news from Brussels, and
while I was hoping to break this to you in person...
well, it's so urgent that I'm not sure we should wait.
It seems that while we were right about the spirit
of 1107/2006, the letter says something different.
Airports are in no way required to provide you with
a wheelchair to use after you go home. It seems
that every other airport in the EU has ensured that
passengers like yourself get home with some sort of
temporary replacement because they've assumed
that's what the regulation said.

The regulation was written in English. So the English
know what they are really saying and what they
aren't. *(Mutters something in Italian)*

Listen, I have to ask you, for the sake of all disabled
passengers across the EU... Stop talking about this.
I know I said make this as loud as you want, but now
we are in trouble. If word got out publicly about
what the reg actually says, it could affect treatment of
passengers across Europe who are like yourself.

I think if you stopped talking about your case, it'll die
away soon enough and those that are being helped,
will keep getting what they need. We're lucky in
that regard. More damage to the status quo could've
easily been done.

There were fifty eight thousand signatures on the petition website,

By the time we took it down.

I asked for an archive of the comments for my own records,

Before the page was cached forever.

I scroll through the document occasionally,

And marvel over how many people,

72

Are asking for help.

Wonder why news hasn't dropped again of someone else in the same situation,

And how many people keep having to bite their tongue,

Waiting,

Hoping it'll work out somehow,

Thinking this cannot possibly be the world we live in.

And yet, the injustice keeps going.

People still ask me,

Whatever happened with that case,

With you and your wheelchair?

You were all over the news for months.

And I tell them,

It settled,

Eventually.

I have a chair,

And life goes on.

Mostly they say in response,

Isn't it nice,

How things always seem to work out,

In the end?

And I know,

I have a reputation among my... friends,

As someone who is out for a fight,

Argumentative,

Intense,

Someone who bats away at people,

But here's my question.

Here's my fucking question to all you people,

Who dare to think that your marathon running,

Paper straw using, conflict dodging way of life is some sort of pinnacle of

Goodwill that shows you really care.

To all you people who wanna look enlightened,

But are scared shitless at the notion that taking a fucking stand

Might mean that someone likes you a little bit less,

When you're old and catch a flight to the Greek Isles,

And your wheelchair gets smashed up in the belly of a plane,

What are you going to do about it?

What are any of you going to do about it?